W9-AGD-472

REGULATORY AGENCIES

A STUDY TEAM REPORT TO
THE TASK FORCE ON
PROGRAM REVIEW

AUGUST, 1985

Available in Canada through

Authorized Bookstore Agents
and other bookstores

or by mail from

Canadian Government Publishing Centre
Supply and Services Canada
Ottawa, Canada   K1A 0S9

Catalogue No. CP 32-50/21-1985E   Canada: $4.75

ISBN 0-660-11991-9   Other Countries: $5.70

Price subject to change without notice

CONTENTS

FOREWORD

The government announced the creation of
the Task Force on Program Review in September,
1984, under the chairmanship of the Deputy Prime
Minister. The other volumes in this series
represent reports which were prepared by mixed
private and public-sector study teams and
considered according to a uniform process which
included review by the Private Sector Advisory
Committee.

At the same time as the Task Force was
created, it was announced that the Deputy Prime
Minister would examine options for reform with
respect to the government's relationship to
regulatory agencies.

This volume represents the work of a
separate study team constituted to accomplish the
review of regulatory agencies and to prepare
proposals for consideration by Cabinet. While
these proposals were not reviewed by the Private
Sector Advisory Committee, the private-public
sector mix of advice was maintained through the
membership of the team and through its
consultation efforts.

The report has been included for release
in the series due to its relationship to the
review of regulatory programs by another study
team and because it also makes proposals to
improve the management of government.

As in all other reports, this volume
represents the first orderly step toward Cabinet
discussion. It does not represent government
policy nor decisions of the government in respect
to any of the options. This report provides the
basis for discussion and a valuable tool in the
decision-making process.

TERMS OF REFERENCE

The objective of the study team is to examine options for reform with respect to the government's relationship to regulatory agencies. The team will recommend options which, in its view, are most likely to:

a.   strengthen the accountability of regulatory agencies;

b.   ensure the degree of competence, impartiality and objectivity that is required to achieve the statutory objectives of regulatory agencies;

c.   minimize adverse effects on the private sector generally and small business in particular, arising from the procedures of regulatory agencies; and

d.   eliminate unnecessary duplication, repetition and waste in dealings between regulatory agencies and the government.

Within the context outlined above, the report of the study team will examine options for reform with respect to the relationship between regulatory agencies and the government (the bureaucracy, the Cabinet, and Parliament). The report will not address options that would involve changes to the content of regulation (e.g. options for deregulation through the removal of particular legal constraints on private sector behaviour), on the ground that such options are more properly handled in the context of separate industry sector policy reviews being conducted by the responsible line Minister. The study team's report will also not address directly the very broad range of regulatory programs being carried out within government departments, which are currently being reviewed by the mixed Study Team on Regulatory Programs.

The study team will rely primarily on two main sources of information: existing studies and reports; and consultations within the government, and with private sector representatives. The team will also draw upon the problem areas identified by the Study Team on Regulatory Programs, with respect to issues concerning the relationship between government and regulatory agencies, as a source of information for its work.

The study team will implement this approach to its task through an examination of options concerning all issues relevant within the context of its objective. Key issues to be addressed include:

a. The appropriateness of having independent regulatory agencies as an organizational model for delivering regulatory programs.

b. The appropriate balance between accountability or regulatory agencies to Cabinet and to Parliament respectively.

c. The appropriateness of various vehicles for agency accountability to Cabinet such as:

   - Policy directives from Cabinet.

   - Cabinet approval of agency decisions.

- Cabinet review of agency decisions.

- Sunset regulation.

- Cabinet review of compliance costs to the private sector.

- Advance notice through agency calendars or agendas.

d. The appropriate methods for evaluating the performance of regulatory agencies.

e. The appropriate procedures for transfer by Cabinet of functions from a regulatory agency to another government body.

f. Issues relating to regulatory procedures, including the appropriate role for public servants as intervenors in the regulatory process.

g. The adequacy of existing policies and procedures or ensuring the accountability of regulatory agencies for the management of their financial and personnel resources.

The study team's report will set out what actions are required in legislation or by Order-in-Council or by other means, if its recommendations are implemented.

Background

Two main factors account for the proliferation of regulatory agencies in recent decades: a dramatic growth in regulatory intervention by governments in the market place; and an increasing use of agencies, rather than government departments or courts, to perform regulatory functions.

Factors commonly cited as having led to the creation of regulatory agencies by Canadian governments are:

- a desire to delegate the responsibility for the resolution of politically sensitive issues to bodies perceived as having a degree of independence from the government;

- the need for a public process, conducted under rules of procedure, to deal with matters involving the adjudication of private rights;

- the need to develop cumulative technical expertise through specialization;

- a reluctance to utilize the courts in matters that, because of their nature or volume, were not considered suitable to the judicial process.

The powers exercised by regulatory agencies are not easily situated within the Canadian political structure, in terms of the balance between independence and accountability. Ours is a system of responsible government where executive functions are performed by ministers who must answer to Parliament for their actions. It is a system where "judicial functions" are exercised by judges, who are insulated from political influence. It is generally agreed that regulatory agencies fit somewhere in between the ministerial and judicial models. However, there is no consensus on the precise degree of independence that regulatory agency decision-making should have from political control. Some are concerned that regulatory agencies, exercising the control over public and private interests that Parliament gives them, may not be held sufficiently accountable politically; others are concerned that political interference with an "independent" agency may compromise the reasons that motivate resorting to this model.

Regulatory agencies have certain common characteristics which distinguish them from government departments. These common characteristics include: collegial decision-making by the agency members; appointment of members on good behaviour for a specified term; a well-structured, often public, decision-making process; and continuity in decision-making, frequently based on precedents. Agencies also have certain characteristics that distinguish them from courts. These include non-adjudicative functions (such as advisory and/or policy-making functions), appointment of non-lawyers as agency members, in some cases more informal procedures, and dealing with a wider range of parties having different levels of interests.

Types of regulatory agencies can be distinguished according to the nature of their functions and the degree of independence which they have for decision-making. Some agencies are limited to the performance of adjudicative functions, while others have policy making functions as well. Some agencies also perform advisory functions. The decisions of some agencies can be overturned by Cabinet as well as

the courts; the decisions of other bodies can be
appealed only to the courts on matters of law or
jurisdiction. The variety that exists in the
types of regulatory agencies reflects the lack of
a consistent rationale for their existence.

Scope

The terms of reference of the study team
require us to advise on options for reform with
respect to the government's relationship with 11
regulatory agencies. These are:

- Atomic Energy Control Board (AECB)

- Canada Labour Relations Board (CLRB)

- Canadian Human Rights Commission (CHRC)

- Canadian Import Tribunal (CIT)

- Canadian Radio-Television and
  Telecommunications Commission (CRTC)

- Canadian Transport Commission (CTC)

- National Energy Board (NEB)

- Public Service Staff Relations Board
  (PSSRB)

- Restrictive Trade Practices Commission
  (RTPC)

- Tariff Board (TB)

- Textile and Clothing Board (TCB)

The focus of our report is on issues of
process. These issues are grouped under six
headings in the following order: control and
accountability for decision-making; regulatory

agency procedures; appointments; administrative controls; other general issues; and agency specific issues.

Our report does not address all of the issues concerned with regulatory reform. As specified in our terms of reference, we do not address options involving the content of regulation (e.g. the elimination of regulatory functions). Such options have been considered by the Study Team on Regulatory Programs and are being addressed in policy reviews being conducted by individual ministers. The administration of regulatory programs by government departments, which has been addressed separately in the report of the Study Team on Regulatory Programs, is also not included within the scope of our report.

Work Approach

The study team was jointly led by a private sector advisor, Mme Louise Martin, partner at Clarkson, Tétrault, and a public sector advisor, Mr. Kenneth Wyman, who are together responsible for this report. The team was assisted by a small staff of public servants and by two private sector representatives (Mr. Louis Caouette of Currie, Coopers and Lybrand and Mr. Laurie Smith of Bennett, Jones). Mr. Dan McCarthy, Executive Assistant to the Deputy Prime Minister, also assisted the work of the study team.

In the preparation of this report the study team relied on three main sources of information: previous studies and reports; consultations with the private sector; and consultations within the government. Previous studies and reports which have been reviewed by the study team include those undertaken by the Economic Council; the Law Reform Commission; the Lambert Commission; the 1981 House of Commons Committee on Regulatory Reform

(Peterson Committee); the 1981 Internal Privy
Council Review Group on Regulatory Reform of Crown
Agencies (PCO Review Group). The team has also
drawn upon relevant portions of the report of the
Study Team on Regulatory Programs.

Our private sector consultation process was
particularly helpful. We consulted with a wide
cross-section of regulated companies, industry
associations, consumer and labour groups, and
individuals having a particular knowledge
pertaining to the issues examined in our report.
A list of the individuals and organizations
consulted in the private sector is included in
this report. Within the government, we have
conducted informal interviews with senior
departmental officials and with the heads of the
11 regulatory agencies listed above.

General Framework

Regulatory agencies in the past have been
established on an ad hoc basis. As noted earlier,
there has been no consistent rationale for their
existence. We believe it is essential to develop
a general framework for defining the basic
principles that should guide the government and
Parliament in deciding when a regulatory agency
should be established and what functions are
appropriate for such an agency. It could also
assist in guiding regulatory agencies in the
performance of their mandates. We are of the view
that such general framework should be set out in
legislation.

In formulating our conclusions with respect
to the content of the proposed general framework
for regulatory agencies, we have given priority to
addressing the concerns that have most frequently
been identified as urgent in our consultation

process, particularly in the private sector. Our conclusions are as follows:

a.   Regulatory agencies should exist only where there is a demonstrated need for intervention in the market place by regulations, and where the agency would conduct regulatory functions more effectively and efficiently than government departments or courts.

b.   The functions that are most likely to be well-suited to the regulatory agency model are functions relating to the adjudication of rights in specific cases, particularly where it can be demonstrated that there is a need to insulate adjudicative decision-making from the political process, and that the nature of the adjudicative functions requires more flexible procedures and/or greater specialized expertise than is normally associated with the courts.

c.   The primary responsibility for policy-making should rest with Parliament and the Cabinet, the elected representatives of the people, not with the appointed members of regulatory agencies. The functions performed by regulatory agencies should be limited as much as possible to adjudication on specific matters, and to the making of regulations which would require the approval of the Governor- in-Council and publication in draft form for public comment.

d.   In the performance of adjudicative functions in specific cases, regulatory agencies should be distinguished from departments in having a considerable degree of independence from government control.

e. Regulatory agencies should be accountable to the government in the same way as departments for the management of their budget.

f. The procedures followed by regulatory agencies should generally be more informal and flexible than those of the courts, and avoid excessive legalization, in order to ensure that costs and delays in the regulatory process are kept to a minimum. The process should provide full opportunity for consultation and participation by regulated companies and other affected interests.

g. The courts should be ultimately responsible to ensure that regulatory agencies do not exceed their mandate as laid down by Parliament. In light of the costliness of the court appeal process, a significant responsibility rests on agency members to ensure that they carry out their mandate in a responsible manner.

CONTROL AND ACCOUNTABILITY FOR DECISION-MAKING

Introduction

There is no consensus regarding the criteria for utilizing a regulatory agency, rather than a government department, to make decisions, enact regulations or perform other functions. Nor, as noted earlier in this report, is there a consensus on the extent of independence from political control that regulatory agencies, once created, should have for decision-making. Nevertheless, based on our consultation process and review of previous studies, the study team believes that there are certain guiding principles, relating to control and accountability for decision-making, that would receive a broad measure of support in the private sector. These guiding principles, which we have taken into account in formulating options for reform to existing control/accountablility regimes for regulatory agencies are as follows:

a. A regulatory agency's objectives and functions must be founded on parliamentary authority, which should be expressed as clearly and with as much precision as possible in the statute that sets up and gives initial instructions to the agency (constituent act).

b. The merits of the regulatory agency model, and the appropriate control/accountability regime for regulatory agency decision-making, depend upon the nature of the functions to be performed. We believe that it is particularly important to distinguish between policy functions, and adjudicative decision-making functions on specific matters within a reasonably precise set of objectives.

c.   Where a regulatory agency is performing adjudicative functions, the study team believes that it is generally preferable to maintain these functions within the regulatory agency, rather than to transfer them to a department. Furthermore, the regulatory agency should be insulated to a considerable extent from political influences in carrying out its adjudicative decision-making functions. The decisions of regulatory agencies, involving the performance of adjudicative functions on specific matters, should be appealable to the courts on matters of law or jurisdiction, but should be independent to a considerable extent from Cabinet control or review. Most of the private sector participants in our consultation process strongly advocated these safeguards. This preference is based on the perception that adjudicative decision-making by an independent regulatory agency will be impartial, in the sense that it will be insulated from political influence, and fair in that it will be carried out by known procedures with an opportunity for participation by interested parties.

d.   Where the statutory mandate of the regulatory agency states its objectives in broad terms, and where the agency therefore has a potentially broad discretion to make policy, Cabinet should, in the view of the study team, have the power to further define the policy framework within which the

regulatory agency exercises its
adjudicative functions, provided that
adequate safeguards are in place to
prevent undue political influence in the
performance of these adjudicative
functions. In support of this
principle, we note three points. First,
the responsibility for broad policy
matters should rest with the elected
representatives of the people, not with
the appointed members of regulatory
agencies. Secondly, the control/
accountability regime to Cabinet should
be more stringent in the case of those
regulatory agencies given broad
discretion to make policy under their
statutory mandates. Thirdly,
significant concerns would arise if
Cabinet controls over policy-making by
regulatory agencies were to
substantially influence decision-making
in specific cases.

Mandatory Periodic Review of Regulatory Agency Statutes

Under our system of parliamentary democracy,
the functions performed by a regulatory agency are
founded on parliamentary authority. As noted
previously, this authority is expressed in the
statute that sets up and gives initial
instructions to the regulatory agency, sometimes
referred to as the agency's "constituent act".
These instructions are sometimes quite specific,
particularly where the regulatory agency is given
only adjudicative functions. For agencies with
broader functions, particularly those of a policy
nature, the initial instructions to a regulatory
agency are sometimes so broad as to amount to
merely requiring it to act in the "public
interest".

15

In the study team's view, the constituent act of each regulatory agency, and its performance under that act, should be subject to a mandatory periodic review by both the government and Parliament. Such a periodic review of the functions and performance of regulatory agencies should be comprehensive and systematic. To ensure this, it should be a statutory requirement imposed on the minister through whom the agency reports to Parliament. The study team, therefore, recommends to the Task Force that the government consider directing that a periodic review be undertaken by the designated minister not less than once every seven years, and the evaluations in support of the review be carried out by the minister through a task force or other appropriate mechanisms where the private sector would be in the majority.

Our observations on the appropriate method that could be followed in such evaluations are stated in "Regulatory Agency Procedures" of this report.

While a mandatory periodic review of the type proposed would not preclude the abolition of a regulatory agency, the study team does not believe that a mandatory periodic review requirement ("sunset review" clause) should include automatic termination of the agency in the absence of re-approval by Parliament ("sunset termination" clause). We believe that a sunset termination clause, as exists in a number of American states, is undesirable because it could lead to an undue increase in the workload of the government or Parliament or to the re-introduction of existing legislation without any systematic evaluation being undertaken. In the study team's view, a statutory requirement for a periodic review and for the tabling of a report on this review in the House of Commons with automatic referral to the appropriate standing committee would address the concern, expressed frequently, that the statutory mandates of regulatory agencies have often outlived their usefulness.

In light of the above, the study team recommends to the Task Force that the government consider that the designated minister be required to undertake a review of the functions and operations of each regulatory agency not less than once every seven years, and further, that a report based on such review be tabled in the House of Commons and be automatically referred to the appropriate standing committee. The study team also would propose that the standing committee have the opportunity to question the minister on the contents of the report, and to obtain (if necessary on an "in camera" basis) studies and data used in its preparation.

Policy Directives

Among the existing regulatory agencies, the CRTC, the CTC, the AECB and the NEB pose special problems of accountability because the objectives in their constituent acts are broadly defined or specify that they pursue competing goals. As a result, these agencies tend to exercise broad discretion and often make policy.

The study team is of the view that Parliament should specify with greater precision the policy objectives of these four agencies. However, it is recognized that in some circumstances such specification may not be possible, particularly where there is a need for flexibility in the statutes to respond to changes in the public policy agenda, and because frequent changes in the constituent acts could put an undue burden on the parliamentary process.

In circumstances where the constituent act gives broad discretion to the regulatory agency, previous reports have suggested provisions allowing the Governor-in-Council to issue directives to the agency on broad policy matters. The study team recognizes that the government has proposed, in Bill C-20, to enable the Governor-in-Council, either on its own motion or at the request of CRTC, to issue to the CRTC a binding direction concerning any matter within the jurisdiction of the Commission. It is also noted that the government's recent discussion paper on transportation proposes that the Governor-in-Council be authorized to issue directions on broad policy matters to the proposed regulatory agency that would replace the CTC.

In private sector consultations, some have supported the view that the Governor-in-Council should be authorized to issue directions on policy matters, particularly in the case of regulatory agencies such as the CRTC, the CTC, the AECB, and the NEB, which have a broad discretion under existing legislation. However, others were concerned that such a direction power could be used to influence the adjudicative functions of agencies in dealing with specific applications. In this regard, it is relevant to note that it is not always easy to make a clear separation between the policy and adjudicative functions performed by certain regulatory agencies because, in practice, the two functions are frequently intertwined.

The study team believes that the merits of a Governor-in-Council direction power must be assessed in relation to the statutory mandates of particular regulatory agencies, and to the safeguards that would be associated with its implementation. The study team is of the view that the direction power could be limited to regulatory agencies with a broad discretion to make policy under their statutory mandate, and introduced only if adequate safeguards are specified in the legislation to prevent undue influence by the government in the adjudicative functions of such agencies. The study team believes such safeguards are essential to respond to concerns expressed in the private sector. In light of the above, the study team recommends to the Task Force that the government consider:

a.   Seeking parliamentary authority empowering the Governor-in-Council to issue directions only to those independent regulatory agencies that have broad mandates to develop and apply policy. Based on the regulatory agencies reviewed in this report, the study team proposes that the Governor-in-Council be empowered to issue directions to the CRTC, the NEB, the AECB, and the CTC or its proposed successor agency. A Governor-in-Council direction power is not proposed for any of the other regulatory agencies reviewed in this report, because their functions are more narrowly adjudicative. Furthermore, there is little support in the private sector for the introduction of a direction power in the case of these agencies.

b.   Limiting Governor-in-Council directions to a regulatory agency to policy matters. The study team recognizes that there is uncertainty as to how the courts would interpret the term "policy". However, in the study team's view this limitation on the Governor-in-Council direction power is justified, in order to address the concern of many in the private sector that a Governor-in-Council direction power not be used to influence the adjudicative functions of a regulatory agency on specific matters.

c.   Introducing a requirement that the full
     text of a policy directive be tabled in
     Parliament for 30 sitting days before it
     comes into effect. This would enable
     Parliament and interested parties in the
     private sector to have an appreciation
     of the contents of the proposed
     directive before it is implemented.

d.   Where a Governor-in-Council direction
     would affect a specific application
     before the regulatory agency, there
     should be a prohibition on the issuance
     of the direction during the period
     between the commencement of a public
     hearing on the application and time of
     making a decision on that application.
     In the view of the study team, this
     safeguard is necessary in order to
     protect the integrity of the
     adjudicative processes of the agency.

e.   Before the commencement of a public
     hearing, the Governor-in-Council should
     be empowered to issue a directive
     requiring the regulatory agency to
     refrain from hearing a specific applica-
     tion for 40 working days. This would
     allow the Governor-in-Council time to
     issue a subsequent directive to the
     regulatory agency on a policy matter
     raised by the application. A refrain
     directive might be seen as undue inter-
     vention by the government in an agency's
     adjudicative processes. However, the
     study team notes that the concept of a
     refrain directive, particularly when
     accompanied by time limits on the issu-
     ance of a subsequent policy directive
     during an agency's hearing and decision-
     making processes, was viewed as a
     reasonable proposal by many participants
     in our consultation process.

Cabinet Powers to Override Agency Decisions

Under present legislation, a Cabinet override power exists only in the case of three regulatory agencies, namely the CRTC, the CTC, and the NEB. With respect to the CRTC, the form of the Cabinet override power differs between broadcasting and telecommunications matters. On the broadcasting side, the Governor-in-Council can refer back or set aside (but not vary) CRTC decisions with respect to the issuance, amendment or renewal of broadcasting licences. On the telecommunications side, the Governor-in-Council can vary or rescind any decision or order of the CRTC. In the case of the CTC, many of the licencing and certification functions are subject to an appeal to the minister, and the Governor-in-Council also has a broad power to vary or rescind any decision, order, rule or regulation of the CTC. In the case of the NEB, the Governor-in-Council is required to approve NEB decisions on pipeline and powerline certificates, and decisions on significant exports and import licences. However, the Governor-in-Council has no authority to override NEB decisions with respect to pipeline tolls and tariffs.

Most private sector participants in our consultation process were of the view that Cabinet override powers are not necessary or appropriate in the case of those regulatory agencies with narrowly-defined adjudicative decision-making functions. There were differences of opinion expressed with respect to whether Cabinet override powers should be retained even in the case of regulatory agencies that are perceived as having broad discretion under existing legislation (the AECB, the CRTC, the CTC, and the NEB). Some believe that the Governor-in-Council should not retain such override powers, particularly if it is given a new power of policy direction over them. Others believe that override powers should be

retained, but that they should be used sparingly
and only in exceptional circumstances. Concerns
were also expressed by several participants
regarding the absence of minimum standardized
procedures for handling Cabinet reviews of
agencies' decisions.

In light of the above, and our review of
previous studies, the study team recommends to the
Task Force that the government consider, with
respect to Cabinet override powers:

a.   That the Governor-in-Council have the
       power to override decisions of the AECB,
       the CRTC, the NEB, and the CTC or its
       proposed successor agency. The present
       provisions for appeals to the courts
       from decisions of these agencies on
       matters of law and jurisdiction could be
       retained. It is proposed that the
       Governor-in-Council not be given the
       power to override decisions of any of
       the other regulatory agencies reviewed
       in this report.

b.   That the override power be uniform for
       the AECB, the CRTC, the NEB, the CTC or
       its proposed successor agency and that
       it be limited to the power to refer back
       or set aside (but not vary) decisions of
       these agencies. This proposal is made
       in the context of our previous proposal
       that the Governor-in-Council be
       authorized to issue policy directives to
       these agencies. In the view of the
       study team, if the proposed policy
       directive power is introduced, the
       retention of the Cabinet override power
       would be justified only if it is limited
       in form, and intended only as a last
       resort fail-safe mechanism of control.

Retention of a Cabinet override power, limited to referring back or setting aside decisions of the four regulatory agencies noted above is, in the view of the study team, the best option to meet these criteria.

c.   Implementing a number of standardized review procedures that would address the process by which Cabinet reviews agency decisions.

1.   When the government intends to review a decision, or when a party applies for review of a decision, notice would be given to all parties of record and to the regulatory agency whose decision is appealed. Notice would be given within 30 days of the rendering of the decision appealed. A party which initiates a review, would be required to send the notice; if review is initiated by the government, it would be required to send the notice.

2.   Parties of record would be allowed 30 days from the time of notice to make written submissions to the Clerk of the Privy Council.

3.   To provide for efficient processing of applications for review the government could decide within 15 days of the receipt of the application and inform the applicant and all parties of record that it will not proceed with review of the decision.

4. A copy of the decision rendered in review by the Governor-in-Council would be sent to every party of record and to the regulatory agency.

Regulation-Making Powers

The power to make regulations for the implementation of their constituent acts is commonplace in the enabling legislation of regulatory agencies. These regulations are typically subject to the approval of the government. However, the CRTC, the CTC, the CLRB and the PSSRB are given authority to make regulations without Governor-in-Council approval. These regulations can have significant policy content.

In the view of the study team, regulations made by agencies should generally be subject to approval by the Governor-in-Council. In this regard, we note the principle articulated by a Special Committee of the House of Commons on Statutory Instruments, which argued that "while independence is the hall-mark of the judicial branch of government, it should be quite alien to the executive branch. The government of the day should be fully responsible to Parliament, and through it to the people for all subordinate laws which are made, whether or not the policy embodied therein was initiated, within the existing departmental structure or elsewhere".*

---

*Canada Parliament, Third Report of the Special Committee on Statutory Instruments, 1968-69, pp. 34, 35.

The study team believes that the requirements under existing legislation for Governor-in-Council approval of regulations made by regulatory agencies should be maintained. Furthermore, in the case of the CRTC, we propose that where it is authorized to make regulations, these be subject to Governor-in-Council approval before being promulgated, with two exceptions: one exception would relate to the CRTC authority to make regulations respecting the proportion of time that may be devoted to the broadcasting of programs, advertisements or announcements of a partisan political character and the assignment of such time on an equitable basis to political parties and candidates (Section 16(1)(b)(iv) of the Broadcasting Act); the other exception relates to the CRTC authority to make regulations respecting the use of dramatization in programs, advertisements or announcements of a partisan political character (Section 16(1)(b)(iv) of the Broadcasting Act). The study team supports the CRTC continuing to have an unfettered authority to make these two specific types of regulations, given their nature.

We also propose that, should the government decide to give any regulation-making authority to the proposed agency to replace the CTC, the exercise of that authority should be made subject to the approval of the Governor-in-Council.

In the case of the PSSRB and the CLRB, we would suggest that these agencies retain their present authority to make regulations without Governor-in-Council approval. In this regard, it is noted that the government as an employer is itself subject to the jurisdiction of the PSSRB. Furthermore, it is noted that a strong preference was expressed in the consultation process, by both employer and labour representatives, that the CLRB be insulated from the political process.

A further issue is whether agencies should be required to publish draft regulations in order to give interested parties an opportunity to make comments on their formulation. Previous reports reviewed by the study team are unanimous that draft regulations should generally be published for this purpose. However, there are differences of view as to whether publication of draft regulations should be made mandatory. Some reports (Standing Joint Committee on Regulations; Ministerial Task Force Study Team on Regulatory Programs), believe that it should be, while other reports (the Peterson Committee and the PCO Review Group) suggest that there could be circumstances where it would not be appropriate to require that regulations be published in advance, depending on such factors as the content of the regulations, the need for quick action, and whether the proposed regulations had minor implications or affected few people.

In the view of the study team, draft publication of regulations made by regulatory agencies is, in most cases, very desirable to encourage input from affected parties and minimize adverse impacts on the private sector. However, as to whether such draft publication should be made mandatory where this is not now a statutory requirement, the study team believes that a distinction could be made between regulations that are subject to Governor-in-Council approval, and those which are not.

In the typical case where agency regulations are subject to Governor-in-Council approval, the study team suggests that draft regulations made by the regulatory agency be published for comment, but that the policy not be made mandatory in all cases. Further, the onus should be on the regulatory agency, when it has not published a draft regulation for comment, to justify why this was not desirable when it forwards the draft regulation to the Governor-in-Council for approval

26

and to the Standing Joint Committee on Regulations and Other Statutory Instruments for scrutiny.

To ensure that a measure of accountability remains where Governor-in-Council approval is not required for regulations made by a regulatory agency, the study team recommends to the Task Force that the government consider that in these circumstances there should be a statutory requirement that a copy of the proposed regulations, or amendments, be published and a reasonable opportunity afforded to affected and interested persons to make representations to the agency in writing prior to the passage of the regulations. This requirement now applies to the regulations of the CRTC under the Broadcasting Act. The study team believes that this should continue to apply to the two types of CRTC regulations where, in the study team's view, Governor-in-Council approval is not appropriate. It is also proposed that the same statutory requirement also apply to regulations of the CLRB and the PSSRB.

When draft regulations are published for comment, or when they are submitted by agencies to Governor-in-Council for approval, agencies should, in the study team's view, be required to provide answers to a minimum set of questions concerning their assessment of the impact of the proposed regulation. It is not suggested that each proposed regulation be accompanied by a rigidly standardized and highly-detailed impact assessment, but that agencies, in seeking comments or approval for proposed regulations, include answers to the following questions:

- What is the problem?

- Why is government intervention necessary?

- What alternative solutions have been
  considered?

- What are the advantages (benefits) and
  disadvantages (costs) of the proposed
  regulation?

- Who will benefit and who will lose from
  this proposal?

- Who has been consulted and what was
  learned?

REGULATORY AGENCY PROCEDURES

Introduction

Previous studies and private sector participants in our consultation process generally agree that regulatory agencies should retain a substantial measure of the flexibility they now have, to develop the procedures that are appropriate in carrying out their specific functions. However, there are also a number of significant general concerns regarding the procedures adopted by regulatory agencies.

Several previous reports have suggested that regulatory agency procedures are generally "too legalistic". Many participants in our private sector consultation process expressed the concern that lawyers often play too prominent a role in agency proceedings, as well as the related concern that the courts or the agencies themselves often impose unnecessarily formal and rigid procedural rules. These are seen as discouraging private citizens from participating in agency proceedings, and creating excessive costs and delay. On the other hand, concern was also expressed by some private sector participants that agency hearings sometimes do not ensure that all relevant facts will be brought before the agency, particularly where there are competing applications. CRTC hearings on competing applications for broadcasting licences were cited as an example where it was suggested that the commission should allow cross-examination.

There is general concern that regulatory agencies are too slow in dealing with applications. It is not uncommon for the decision-making process to be subject to considerable delays, extending into many months or, in some cases, even years. Such delays are seen as unacceptable. They create uncertainty, raise the costs of attracting capital for regulated companies, and result in less investment and job creation. As noted in the report of the Study Team on Regulatory Programs, such time delays are especially intolerable "in instances of economic regulation where technology, information and markets move too quickly for the 19th century decision-making traditions".

Hearing Procedures

In the study team's view, regulatory agencies, in carrying out most of their functions, should be encouraged to implement informal and less legalistic procedures, and not be forced by the courts to adopt rigid procedural rules so long as they observe the principles of fairness. However, the study team also believes that agencies should adopt more formal procedures when the agency's function is to adjudicate between competing applications for a right or privilege or where persons are in jeopardy of losing rights or privileges already enjoyed (such as the revocation or suspension of a licence).

In light of the above, the study team recommends to the Task Force that the government consider:

a. Giving each agency the discretion to determine first whether to hold a hearing on any application, and second to determine whether it should be an "oral" or "paper" hearing, except that where there are competing applications for a right or privilege or where persons are in jeopardy of losing rights or privileges already enjoyed, the

agency would be obligated to hold an
oral public hearing.

b.   When an agency has an oral public
      hearing, giving it the discretion to
      determine whether cross-examination is
      allowed, except that parties should have
      the express right to cross-examination
      where there are competing applications
      for a right or privilege or where a
      party is in jeopardy of losing a right
      or privilege already enjoyed.

c.   Indicating in each agency's statute that
      it is the duty of the agency to deal
      with all matters coming before it as
      informally and expeditiously as the
      circumstances and considerations of
      fairness permit. To allow the agency to
      fulfil this duty it would not be bound
      by legal rules of evidence in conducting
      a hearing except where there are
      competing applications for a right or
      privilege or where a party is in
      jeopardy of losing a right or privilege
      already enjoyed.

d.   Giving each agency the express power to
      hold pre-hearing conferences to decide
      procedural matters, seek admissions from
      parties, require the production of
      evidence which in its view is necessary
      and indicate whether it will accept to
      hear evidence on certain matters.

Time Limits

    In the view of the study team, regulatory
agencies should retain considerable flexibility to
determine the time periods for dealing with

applications. However, in light of the widespread concerns about the slowness of agency decision-making processes, some statutory limits on agency discretion in this area are justified.

Accordingly, the study team proposes to the Task Force that the government consider a statutory requirement that each regulatory agency by regulation establish maximum time limits for those classes of applications which it processes and for each of the different stages in the processing of these applications. The maximum time limits proposed by each agency should be subject to the approval of the Governor-in-Council. In the view of the study team, regulatory agencies should also be allowed to apply to the Governor-in-Council for exemptions from such time limits where they can demonstrate that such limitations are not feasible for certain types of applications.

The study team recognizes that even the establishment of effective time limits for dealing with applications will not necessarily be sufficient to ensure adherence on a consistent basis by each agency. In this regard, the study team suggests that each regulatory agency be required, in its annual report to Parliament, to identify all cases where the established time limits have not been complied with, and to state the reasons for such non-compliance in that report.

Cost Awards

Among federal regulatory agencies, only the CTC and the CRTC (with respect to telecommunications matters) have the power to award costs. In practice, only the CRTC has made use of this power.

In the view of the study team, it is necessary to distinguish between two purposes for enabling regulatory agencies to award costs. The first purpose relates to the awarding of costs against regulated companies as means of funding formal participation in such proceedings. This is the purpose for which the CRTC has used its power to award costs in telecommunications rate cases. The second purpose for cost awards relates to the award of such costs against any party, as a means of penalizing abuses to the regulatory agency process.

Previous reports are divided on the merits of giving regulatory agencies the discretion to award costs for the purpose of funding intervenors to regulatory proceedings. The Peterson Committee recommended that the CRTC's practice of awarding costs to certain public interest groups should be expanded, and that the government should take the necessary steps to permit other regulatory agencies to award costs for this purpose. However, the 1981 PCO Review Group opposed the awarding of costs against regulated companies as a means of funding intervenors, recommending as an alternative that four regulatory agencies (the NEB, the CTC, the AECB, and the CRTC) should be given funds by the government for a four-year experimental period to fund certain intervenors.

In our consultation process, views were divided on the use of cost awards to fund intervenors to regulatory agency proceedings. One private sector participant opposed government assistance by any mechanism, including cost awards, for this purpose. Several others contended that the government, rather than regulatory agencies, should be responsible for providing funding assistance. Others -- particularly representatives of consumer and public interest groups -- support cost awards to intervenor groups as a useful supplement to

whatever core funding is provided by the
government to such groups.

Several industry participants in our
consultation process contended that regulatory
agencies, like the courts, should have the power
to use cost awards to discourage irresponsible
applications or interventions. The Canadian Human
Rights Commission was cited as a particular
example by several private sector participants
where a cost award mechanism was seen as
potentially useful for this purpose.

In light of the above, the study team
recommends to the Task Force that the government
consider, with respect to whether regulatory
agencies should have the discretion to award costs
in their proceedings:

     a.   That regulatory agencies not have the
         power to award costs against regulated
         companies for the purpose of funding
         intervenors. If funding assistance is
         to be provided to intervenors, the study
         team believes that it is more fair that
         taxpayers, rather than the shareholders
         or customers of regulated companies,
         bear the costs of such assistance. The
         practice of awarding costs against
         regulated companies as a means of
         funding interventions has sometimes been
         defended on the grounds that the
         regulated companies can pass these costs
         on to their customers. However, we note
         that it may not be feasible for
         regulated companies to pass such costs
         on to their customers, particularly in
         competitive markets. Furthermore, the
         study team believes that the government,
         not regulatory agencies, should be
         responsible for the essentially
         political decision of determining

whether it is necessary in the pursuit
of equity and in the interests of
balanced decision-making by agencies, to
provide funding assistance to groups or
individuals who are less well-financed
than regulated companies to prepare and
present their views to regulatory
agencies.

b.   Giving regulatory agencies the
discretion to award costs against any
party, for the purpose of discouraging
clear cases of abuse of the regulatory
process. Cost awards for this purpose
may be seen by some as an unwarranted
limitation on the public process that is
an integral and valuable part of the
regulatory agency process, and as an
unnecessary substitute for the role of
the panel chairman in controlling abuses
of that process. However, the study
team believes that such cost awards
would strengthen the public process, by
encouraging parties to exercise
reasonable self-discipline in hearings,
thereby helping to address the concerns
that many private sector participants in
our consultations have raised regarding
the slowness and costliness of
regulatory agency proceedings.

Other Procedural Issues

a.   Departmental Officials as Intervenors

It is not the general practice for
government officials to appear before agencies,
although they may have valuable information to
contribute. The study team recommends to the Task
Force that the government consider encouraging
government officials to appear before regulatory

agencies to speak to the facts at issue,
especially when agencies are engaged in hearings
related to general issues rather than particular
applications. The study team further proposes
that the role of departmental officials as
intervenors stop short of policy statements of any
kind. It should be noted that these proposals
were generally supported by private and public
sector participants in our consultations; they
were also made by the 1981 PCO Review Group.

b.   'He Who Hears - Decides' Rule

When an agency holds a public hearing, a
panel of members is normally selected by the
chairman of the agency for the hearing.
Furthermore, the members of the panel generally
make the decisions on matters heard, based on the
'he who hears-decides' rule. In the view of the
study team, this is usually the fairest way of
making decisions following a public hearing. We
suggest that the 'he who hears-decides' rule be
the general principle for agency decisions, unless
there are compelling circumstances to the
contrary. At the same time, the study team
believes that the chairman of the agency should be
able to determine how many members are on a
hearing panel, and which ones. We also propose
that the chairman of each regulatory agency be
given express powers in the statute to select the
members of such panels.

c.   Reasons for Decisions

Several private sector participants in
our consultations have cited examples of certain
regulatory agencies which, in some cases, do not
give adequate reasons for their decisions. The
study team recommends to the Task Force that the
government consider requiring each regulatory
agency to give meaningful reasons for every

decision made with respect to an application heard at a public hearing. Discretion could be given to each regulatory agency to render such reasons in writing or verbally, and the agency could be expressly allowed to give combined reasons for decisions on a number of applications involving substantially the same issues. The study team also proposes that agency decisions following a public hearing identify members who concur with the decision and those who dissent, together with meaningful reasons for their dissent.

APPOINTMENTS

Introduction

Because the quality of appointments to
regulatory agencies so directly affects the
quality and timeliness of decisions they make, the
subject of appointments has been a major theme in
several previous reports on regulatory reform and
in our consultations for this report. A number of
participants in our consultations criticized the
lack of competence of members of certain
regulatory agencies. A major issue related to the
number of agency members with sufficient "hands
on" business background and knowledge of the
industries regulated by particular agencies. We
also note the observation made by the Study Team
on Regulatory Programs, that "there was frequent
private sector comment on perceived shortcomings
in the appointments to some regulatory agencies.
Criticisms were made about the occasional lack of
(1) expertise, (2) merit, or (3)
representativeness..."

The study team recognizes that the
appointments process for regulatory agency members
is based on the prerogative of the Prime Minister,
and that it is part of the system for
order-in-council appointments generally.
Proposals regarding the appointments process are
made within this context. They relate to the
following areas: The length and conditions of
appointment; the appointments process;
Parliamentary review of agency appointments;
remuneration and benefits; and training for agency
members.

Length and Conditions of Appointments

The appropriate duration and security of appointments to agencies depends on a number of factors. As regards the duration of appointments, views expressed in our consultations were far from unanimous. The majority of those consulted favoured appointments of four to five years in length, which was regarded as a reasonable time period for attracting good candidates while at the same time maintaining reasonable flexibility for the government to appoint fresh minds and replace others. Some private sector participants would favour shorter maximum time periods of not more than two to three years.

Most participants in our consultations were of the view that agency members should be removable only for cause, rather than at pleasure. Quasi-judicial and regulatory functions are generally regarded as ones which justify the greater security of tenure associated with removal for cause.

The study team proposes that an appropriate balance between security and flexibility can be struck by uniform statutory provisions that full-time appointments to regulatory agencies be for fixed terms not exceeding five years, that these terms be renewable for one fixed term not to exceed five years, and that the chairman as well as other members be removable only for cause. The study team also proposes that regular part-time members (not temporary members) be similarly treated but that the maximum term of office be three years.

The maximum terms suggested above are shorter than those specified in several existing statutes, and would provide the government with more flexibility. Under existing statutes, the AECB is the only regulatory agency which was reviewed whose members are presently appointed at pleasure. In the case of two agencies (the NEB and the CHRC), the dismissal of members under their present statutes requires a joint resolution in both Houses of Parliament. In the study team's view, these requirements are unnecessarily rigid. The study team proposes that they be changed to conform with other regulatory agencies.

Appointments Process

With respect to the appointments process, the study team makes the following observations:

a. A common concern of private sector participants in the consultations is that not enough people with business experience have been appointed in the past to agencies which regulate business. We understand that the present government is giving high priority to addressing this concern in relation to order-in-council appointments generally, by such techniques as greater use of executive search firms, talent banks, and consultations with appropriate industry representatives. It is also difficult to attract a greater number of competent business people while ensuring that there are no real or apparent conflicts of interest in the appointment of agency members.

b. Several participants in the consultation process suggested that Ministers consult with the head of an agency to which an appointment is to be made to obtain

views on the qualities and expertise
needed at that period in time. A
similar view was expressed in the report
of the 1981 PCO Review Group. The study
team recognizes that the government must
determine under what circumstances it
may be appropriate to consult with
agency heads concerning the appointment
of members, and if so, in what manner.
We believe that it would generally be
appropriate for Ministers to consult
with agency heads on the qualities and
expertise needed and, if the Minister
wishes, to discuss potential candidates.

Parliamentary Review of Regulatory Agency Appointments

The recent Report of the Special Committee on
Reform of the House of Commons (Honourable J.A.
McGrath, Chairman) was of the view that
order-in-council appointments to the CRTC, the
CTC, and the NEB, should require not only that
names be submitted to the appropriate Committee of
the House of Commons, but that an adverse report
from the committee should constitute a veto of the
nomination. In the committee's view such a degree
of parliamentary review over appointments to these
agencies is justified because of the influence
which they have in substantial policy making, and
because the executive has little control over
their decisions.

Views expressed in the study team's consultation process were about evenly divided regarding
the merits of parliamentary review of order-in-
council appointments to regulatory agencies. Some
contended that such a process would be desirable,
while others expressed concern that it could be
superficial and partisan and would therefore
discourage competent individuals from allowing
their names to stand as potential nominees.

The study team notes that the government has recently announced its intention to allow parliamentary scrutiny of certain order-in-council appointments, and that such scrutiny would not include the power to veto appointments. In the study team's view, if regulatory agency appointments are to be subject to such review, it will be important to ensure insofar as possible that the review process focusses on matters relevant to assessing the competence of the nominee, and that it is conducted in a responsible and non-partisan manner.

Remuneration and Benefits

As noted above, a number of participants in the consultation process expressed concern that not enough people with business experience are appointed to regulatory agencies. A related concern is that the existing levels of remuneration and benefits are not high enough to attract such qualified people to regulatory agencies. The study team believes that this issue is appropriately addressed within the broader context of studies on compensation for order-in-council appointments generally.

Training for Agency Members

Most agency heads, and others who were consulted, believe that the best training for members is generally on-the-job training. Furthermore, the study team notes that agency members, if interested, can participate in relevant courses offered at universities or in the government. However, in the view of the study team, there is sufficient concern regarding the lack of agency members with specialized training in certain areas (e.g. how to conduct public hearings, decision-writing, media relations, regulatory procedures) to warrant the

establishment of an appropriate focal point in the
government to explore, in consultation with agency
persons, the desirability of developing additional
courses specially to meet these needs. In the
view of the study team, any such courses would
preferably be offered outside the government.

ADMINISTRATIVE CONTROLS

Accountability for Management

As noted previously, regulatory agencies are generally distinguishable from government departments in having a degree of independence with respect to decision-making, which is typically exercised through the board or commission form of collegial decision-making by members who are appointed for a fixed term and removable only 'for cause'.

In contrast, regulatory agencies under existing legislation are not, in general, distinguishable from government departments with respect to administrative controls over such matters as budgeting. The study team sees no reason why this situation should be altered. The case for agency autonomy with respect to adjudicative decision-making does not apply with the same force to the administration or management of these agencies in the view of the study team.

Most of the statutes establishing regulatory agencies clearly designate one official (typically the chairman of the agency) as chief executive officer having responsibility for management of the agency. However, as noted by the Lambert Commission, there are certain regulatory agencies (namely the Canadian Transport Commission and the Tariff Board) where no such position is designated or it is ambiguous where such responsibility rests. The study team shares the view of the Lambert Commission that accountability for administration demands that responsibilities be clearly assigned and that a chief executive officer of the regulatory agency be clearly recognized. Accordingly, the study team proposes that every constituent act of a regulatory agency designate one official as chief executive officer who will be responsible for the supervision and direction of the work and staff of the agency and be held responsible for the administration of the agency.

Personnel Controls

Regulatory agencies are presently subject to a significant number of controls relating to such personnel matters as total authorized person-years, the distribution of such person-years to particular classification groups, classification levels, re-deployment of personnel, and the criteria on which staff can be dismissed. The study team recognizes that personnel controls imposed on regulatory agencies are at present not different from those imposed on government departments. It is also noted that the question of whether such controls are excessively rigid, and could be replaced by a more flexible regime limited to overall budgetary controls and the monitoring of results, raises issues that are common to both regulatory agencies and government departments. Nevertheless, the study team wishes to express concern, based on representations made in the consultation process, that the present regime of personnel controls may be too rigid, and that it may be inhibiting the flexibility of agencies to carry out their responsibilities in an effective and cost-efficient manner.

Common Support Services

Regulatory agencies generally are smaller than departments while still requiring a basic level of support services, such as personnel, financial, library and administrative services. Over at least the last 15 years, several proposals have been made by Treasury Board and Supply and Services Canada officials to establish a pool of common support services for smaller agencies.

None of these proposals have been implemented, although a few agencies use the support services of their host department. In the past, agencies have generally resisted the development of a common support services organization on two main grounds: first, that their independence is compromised by not having complete control over their support services; secondly, that their support services are so specialized that they cannot adequately be provided from a central source.

The study team recognizes that the above-noted concerns may have some validity. However, they might be diminished to a considerable extent if the agencies were given the discretion either to maintain in-house support services, or to purchase services on a cost-recovery basis from a common support organization in the event that one is established.

In light of the above, the study team recommends to the Task Force that the government consider directing Treasury Board, in consultation with regulatory agencies and Supply and Services Canada, to further explore the feasibility of establishing common support services for regulatory agencies.

Budgetary Process and Agency Direction

In its report, the Lambert Commission opposed the use of the budgetary approval process to control the policies and direction of regulatory agencies and other independent deciding bodies, stating as follows:

"Subtle pressures ... can be exerted by departments and central agencies on deciding bodies through the Treasury Board budget approval process. While we endorse the approval of budgets as an important part of the management and financial accountability process, we do not believe that the budget approval process is an appropriate instrument for controlling the policies and direction of independent deciding bodies..." (p. 313-314).

The study team supports the Lambert Commission's view that the budgetary process is not an appropriate instrument for controlling the policies and direction of regulatory agencies. Other means have been proposed in this report for strengthening legislative/executive controls over the direction of agencies, including mandatory periodic reviews of agency mandates and functions, strengthened executive powers regarding regulation-making and policy directions for certain agencies, certain procedural controls under legislation, and shorter order-in-council appointments to certain agencies. In the study team's view, these are more appropriate than the budgetary process to exercise necessary controls over regulatory agencies without impairing their independence in the performance of functions required under their statutes.

Paper Burden

Many private sector participants in the consultation process expressed concern at what they regard as unnecessary forms and paper burden imposed by regulatory agencies, as well as by departments that are responsible for the delivery of regulatory programs. In response to this concern, the study team recommends to the Task Force that the government consider the establishment of a focal point in an appropriate central agency, where prior approval would be required for the issuance of forms by an agency requiring information from the private sector. Such a focal point exists in the Office of

Management and Budget in the United States, and it has had some success in controlling what many in the private sector regard as a major irritant and expense.

OTHER GENERAL ISSUES

Parliamentary Estimates Approval Process and Annual Reporting

Currently, the main contact between regulatory agencies and Parliament occurs during the annual approval of spending estimates. Previous reports and most participants in our consultations are of the view that the present process of estimates approval is an unsatisfactory means for assessing the overall performance of regulatory agencies. The study team believes that Parliament's role in holding regulatory agencies accountable for the overall performance of their responsibilities could be improved significantly by regular assessments through the appropriate standing committees, in the context of the estimates approval process.

In order to facilitate such parliamentary assessments, the study team recommends to the Task Force that the government consider having the annual reports of regulatory agencies be automatically referred to the appropriate standing committees of the House of Commons; that these reports provide:

- a thorough description of the agency's activities of the previous year including achievements, shortcomings and problems;

- a record of decisions issued;

- policy directives received and a description of how they have been dealt with; and

- plans and priorities for the coming year.

The study team also proposes that such annual reports identify functions which the agency has the discretion to carry out (but which it is not required to perform under its statutory mandate) and provide a thorough description and justification for any such discretionary functions it has performed in the previous year or intends to perform in the future. The study team notes also an earlier proposal that maximum time limits should be established for different types of applications and that each agency in its annual report be required to identify cases of and reasons for such non-compliance with the time limits.

In the view of the study team, regular Parliamentary assessments conducted by the standing committees supported by more informative annual reports would assist in building a foundation for a mandatory periodic review of agency mandates and functions, as proposed earlier in this report, that the government and Parliament should undertake for each agency not less than once every seven years.

Transfer of Powers

In 1977, the government proposed in Bill C-33 that the Cabinet be empowered to transfer any statutory function of the Canadian Transport Commission, except its licencing and rate-controlling powers, from the agency to the Minister of Transport. Insofar as regulatory agencies are concerned, the study team concurs with the Lambert Commission's recommendation that, without abrogating the powers granted to the Governor-in-Council in the Public Service Rearrangement and Transfer of Duties Act, the transfer to a department or agency of government of any function assigned by statute to such regulatory agency should require parliamentary approval.

Evaluating Agency Performance

Under our terms of reference, the study team has been directed to address the issue of the appropriate methods for evaluating the performance of regulatory agencies. The issue has been addressed primarily in relation to the type of evaluation that could be done in support of the mandatory comprehensive review of each regulatory agency proposed previously. Within this context, the study team makes the following observations:

a. That credible evaluations of the performance of agencies must generally be done externally, and with substantial input from the private sector (broadly defined to include not only the regulated companies, but also groups and individuals affected by agency decisions and regulations). In the team's view, feedback from agency "clientele" is crucial in evaluating agency performance.

b. That successful evaluation of agency performance requires a clear identification of the objectives against which performance is to be assessed. As noted previously, the statutes for certain regulatory agencies do not provide such a clear statement of objectives. Nor, as the report of the Study Team on Regulatory Programs has observed, has there been articulated an overall regulatory policy setting out principles for using regulation as an instrument of public policy.

c. Following the identification of objectives, the results of regulation should be identified, measured and compared to the extent possible with the results that would have occurred in the absence of regulation.

d. In assessing the effectiveness of agency performance, it is crucial to evaluate not only any benefits which may be identified as arising from the results of regulation in relation to the agency's objectives but also estimate the total costs associated with the operation of the regulatory agency, including the direct and indirect costs imposed on the private sector by agency decisions and regulations. In practice, the study team believes that the most important gaps in the government's existing evaluation information with respect to regulatory agencies relates to the lack of information concerning such costs imposed on the private sector.

e. In addition to assessing effectiveness, evaluation of agency performance should also include an assessment of its efficiency, not only in terms of minimizing operating costs but also in terms of whether its process is perceived as fair.

Recovery of Agency Costs

In the view of the study team, enhanced cost recovery should not generally be applied in the particular case of regulatory agencies. Two of the conditions often cited to justify enhanced cost recovery are:

a. the demand for the service provided by the organization is discretionary from the standpoint of the users; and

b. the organization providing the service is actually or potentially in competition with the private sector.

These conditions are obviously not met in the case of the adjudicative and rule making functions performed by the regulatory agency. The regulated company does not have the discretion to choose whether these functions should be performed; it is compelled by statute to comply with agency decisions and regulations.

The study team believes that a case can be made for recovery of costs in circumstances where regulated groups derive direct benefits from services provided by the agency, such as the provision of research and data services, particularly where the user has the discretion to purchase such services and where an actual or potential alternative exists in the private sector.

The Provision of Agency Advice to the Government

In many instances, the various regulatory agencies are empowered by their constituent statutes to give advice to the minister or the government on matters within their mandate when requested to do so. In certain circumstances, it may be of considerable value for the minister or the government to be able to refer issues to agencies for public hearing and report. While care is needed to avoid conflict with the adjudicative functions of agencies, the study team believes that such a power should be provided to the government in view of its potential value.

Accordingly, the study team recommends to the Task Force that the government consider impowering the minister or Governor-in-Council, in appropriate cases, to require agencies to initiate public hearings to inquire into, hear and report on all matters within the agency's jurisdiction, including the agency's own internal operations and procedures. The study team further proposes that in each case, the terms of reference for the subject and conduct of the hearing, its procedures and the conditions of the release of the agency's report should be at the discretion of the minister or Governor-in-Council.

However, it is important to distinguish the request of advice by the government from a statutory right on the part of the agency to give advice on its own initiative, such as now exists for the NEB under the National Energy Board Act and for the CTC under the National Transportation Act. The study team suggests that it is not appropriate to provide such a right by statute because the provision of advice from the agency to the government should be at the initiative of the government and not that of the agency. Accordingly, the study team recommends to the Task Force that the government consider eliminating these statutory rights for the CTC and the NEB.

AGENCY SPECIFIC ISSUES

AECB: Composition of the Board and Public Hearings

a.   Board Composition

The primary roles of the Atomic Energy Control Board are set out in the Atomic Energy Control Act, first enacted in 1946. It authorizes the AECB to regulate and control atomic energy materials and equipment in the interests of safety and physical welfare, to control atomic energy materials, equipment and information in the interests of national security and to promote atomic energy research.

Since 1946, the AECB has been comprised of one full-time President and four part-time members. Since the original Atomic Energy Control Act was passed, the range of problems and issues dealt with by the AECB has expanded considerably with the growth in nuclear reactors and applications of nuclear technology. Representatives from the nuclear industry consulted by the study team were in agreement that an expansion in the number of full-time members of the board is warranted. They suggested that board members often do not have sufficient time to devote to board issues and, that in some cases, board staff may play an unduly large role. The study team notes that this issue has also been addressed by the Law Reform Commission, and by the Study Team on Regulatory Programs.

In light of these concerns, the study team believes that a strong case can be made to expand the number of full-time members of the AECB. Moreover, an expansion in the number of full-time members could provide an opportunity for

broadening representation on the board (some
criticism was expressed in our consultation
process on the preponderance of academics on the
board). Accordingly, we agree with the view of
the Study Team on Regulatory Programs that the
Minister of Energy, Mines and Resources should
review the structure of the AECB and expand the
number of members to include more permanent
members representing industry, labour and public
interests. The study team also suggests that such
a review address whether there would be a need in
an expanded board to retain any part-time members.

   b.   Public Hearings

         Unlike other regulatory agencies, the
AECB does not hold public hearings on a regular
basis. The views expressed in our consultation
process on this matter were divided.
Representatives of the regulated utilities and
AECB contend that the present process, largely
closed to the public, provides the proper
non-adversarial forum for the resolution of highly
technical issues regarding nuclear safety
standards. Furthermore, they are concerned that
the introduction of an extensive public hearing
process could lead to the development of a more
detailed and prescriptive approach to regulation,
as in the United States. It is contended that the
Canadian approach to nuclear safety has
traditionally been less prescriptive than the
American (although there has been increasingly
detailed regulation of the uranium mining industry
in recent years), and that Canada's approach has
achieved good results in terms of protecting
public safety.

         Others the study team consulted,
particularly representatives from public interest
groups, are very critical of the AECB's lack of
public hearings. They criticize the board for not
maintaining an arm's length relationship with

industry and contend that greater reliance on public hearings need not degenerate into the highly polarized, adversarial, and lengthy proceedings that have sometimes occurred in the United States. They also reject the view that matters of nuclear safety are purely technical, best left in the hands of experts and advisory committees.

In the view of the study team, it would not be appropriate to amend the legislation to require the AECB to hold hearings in any types of cases. We believe that the AECB should continue to have the discretion to decide when to hold a public hearing. At the same time, the AECB should be directed to review the manner in which its discretion is presently being carried out with a view to identifying possible types of applications where a public hearing process would be justified, and, if so, based on what procedures. Accordingly, the study team recommends to the Task Force that the government consider directing the AECB to hold a public hearing to review the manner in which it uses its discretion in relation to the procedures followed with respect to different types of applications.

CRTC: Regional Decentralization, Part-Time Members, and Broadcasting Decision-Making Powers

a.   Regional Decentralization

During our consultations, several representatives expressed concern at the degree of regional alienation regarding the CRTC, particularly in Western Canada. In the view of the study team, such alienation is due to a number of factors, not all of which are under commission control. However, the study team believes that the CRTC can -- and should -- make its operations more regionally sensitive.

In this regard, the study team noted that the commission itself has been considering proposals to expand the number of regional staff offices from four to six, and to expand the role of regional staff with respect to participation in the public hearing process, processing of certain types of applications, provision of information, and handling of complaints and inquiries. However, the study team understands that progress to date has been slow in implementing these proposals, because of budgetary and staff constraints.

It is the view of the study team that high priority should be given to regional decentralization at the commission staff level. Accordingly, the study team recommends to the Task Force that the government consider whether means can be found to proceed on an accelerated basis with implementation of regional decentralization at the CRTC staff level, consistent with existing levels of resources.

A further and much more far-reaching issue relates to whether it would be desirable to decentralize some of the CRTC's broadcasting decision-making functions (and if so, which ones) to regionally based panels of full-time commissioners who could be resident in each region. The study team recommends to the Task Force that the government consider whether regional decentralization of some of the CRTC's broadcasting decision-making functions would be feasible, taking into account potential benefits in terms of reducing regional alienation and potential disadvantages in terms of the impact on the consistency and coherence of agency decision-making across the country.

b.   Part-Time Members

        Currently, the CRTC is composed of nine
full-time members including the chairman, two
vice-chairmen, and six other commissioners who
together comprise the Executive Committee. In
addition, there are 10 part-time members of the
commission. Under the Broadcasting Act, the
Executive Committee makes decisions on all
broadcasting licensing matters (except
revocation), but it must consult with the
part-time members in attendance at a meeting of
the full Commission. In addition, the approval of
the part-time members as well as the full-time
members, is required for the making of regulations
by the CRTC applicable to all persons holding
broadcasting licences.

        The principal rationale for having part-time
members in the CRTC is to represent the public
regionally and to feed back to the CRTC those
views and opinions as expressed by Canadians on
broadcasting matters. This is a view rejected by
industry representatives who are of the view that
the requirements that 10 part-time members must be
consulted on all broadcasting matters results in a
more cumbersome and lengthy CRTC decision-making
process.

        The study team recommends to the Task Force
that the government consider eliminating the
part-time category of member for the CRTC.
Alternatively, the government should consider
exploring the merits of two other options: (a)
limiting the role of the part-time members to
voting only on matters pertaining to their region,
and which have been heard at a public hearing in
which they have participated; (b) the same as
option (a), except that part-time members would
have only the right to be consulted.

c.   'He Who Hears - Decides' Rule

        The CRTC, alone among regulatory
agencies, does not follow the 'he who hears-
decides' rule. Under the Broadcasting Act, the
Executive Committee (or in some cases the Full
Commission) must decide on all broadcasting
matters, whether they have heard the application
or not. In the study team's view, there is an
element of unfairness in permitting members who
have not participated in a hearing to share in the
decision-making. Furthermore, the requirement
that 10 -- or 19 -- members of the Commission
must make the decisions is an additional factor
contributing to what many perceive to be the
slowness of the CRTC's decision-making processes
on the broadcasting side. However, the study team
recognizes that where major policy issues are
involved, there may be some advantages in having
the Executive Committee or the Full Commission
make decisions.

        In light of the above, the study team
recommends to the Task Force that the government
consider reviewing the CRTC's decision-making
powers on the broadcasting side, with a view to
determining whether the legislation should be
amended to adopt the 'he who hears-decides' rule
for broadcasting matters.

CLRB: Composition of the Board

        In its report, the Study Team on Regulatory
Programs noted that both industry and labour
groups agreed on the need for this agency, but
expressed concern that the CLRB's procedures are
lengthy and too often legalistic. Furthermore,
the report stated that a major industry and a
labour group both indicated a need to make the
composition of the board more representative, in

order to emphasize practicality rather than the current legalistic/procedural context.

The study team has an additional concern, which we believe could be addressed within the context of the government's relationship to the CLRB. In our consultation process, we were struck by the dichotomy in views of employer and labour representatives concerning the CLRB. Employer representatives -- both large and small -- were critical of the CLRB, expressing the view that its decisions are generally interventionist in favour of labour. The labour representatives interviewed generally regarded the CLRB as being fair, although there were criticisms of excessively legalistic and lengthy procedures.

The adjudication of labour disputes is a complex and difficult area, and CLRB decicions will inevitably be viewed differently by different parties to disputes. Nevertheless, the apparent imbalance between employer and labour perceptions of the CLRB suggests that there may be a need for the government to review the composition of the CLRB. In this context, the study team notes, that since 1973, the full-time members of the CLRB have been non-representational (largely industrial relations practitioners and some lawyers). We also note that a Law Reform Commission study paper published in 1980 and the report of the Study Team on Regulatory Programs have both identified the option of changing the composition of the board to a representative model that would be similar to that adopted by a number of provincial labour relations boards.

The study team recommends to the Task Force that the government consider exploring the merits of the representative model for the CLRB in light of the concerns identified both in our report and in the report of the Study Team on Regulatory Programs.

PSSRB: Costs and Cost Recovery

The mandate of the PSSRB is to administer the 1967 Public Service Staff Relations Act which established a system of collective bargaining and grievance adjudication in the Federal Public Service. The constituency regulated by the PSSRB includes approximately 216,000 government employees. By comparison, CLRB's constituency, which is based on the Canada Labour Code, applies to approximately 600,000 employees in private sector companies and certain crown corporations which are subject to federal jurisdiction.

The cost of administering the PSSRB in 1984 was approximately $50.00 per person employed in the Public Service, which was about five times greater than the per capita cost of administering the CLRB. To a considerable extent, this difference in costs reflects the fact that the PSSRB performs certain functions which are not performed by the CLRB, including the Pay Research Bureau, the provision of mediation and conciliation services, and more extensive grievance adjudication functions. The Pay Research Bureau alone accounts for about 40 per cent of the PSSRB's budget, with expenditures of about $3.9 million in 1984-1985.

Integrating the PSSRB and the CLRB into a single labour relations board might generate some administrative cost savings compared with the present situation. However, we do not favour this option under present legislation. In the study team's view, any administrative cost savings are likely to be minor and to be greatly outweighed by the disadvantages of integration. In this regard, employer and labour representatives in our consultation process -- both private and public -- were generally opposed to integration of the two boards under present legislation. It is possible

that such opposition could be minimized to some
extent if separate committees were established to
regulate public sector and private sector labour
relations respectively within an integrated
board. But in the view of the study team,
opposition from most employer and labour groups to
any form of integrated board is likely to remain
considerable, as long as the statutory mandates
and collective bargaining regimes under which
public and private sector employees operate
continue to differ significantly.

As noted, approximately 40 per cent of the
PSSRB's expenditures are accounted for by the Pay
Research Bureau. The bureau conducts research and
carries out surveys that provide comparisons on
rates of pay and working conditions for comparable
occupations in the public and private sector. The
services offered by the Pay Research Bureau are
utilized by the employer and labour groups for
collective bargaining purposes.

Presently, no charge is paid by the users of
the Pay Research Bureau who benefit from its
services. For the reasons stated in "Other
General Issues" of this report, the study team
believes that the policy of cost recovery should
generally be implemented with caution for
regulatory agencies. However, in the case of the
Pay Research Bureau, the users have the discretion
as to whether to participate in the services
provided by the bureau, or whether to seek other
sources of data for collective bargaining
purposes. Labour representatives in our
consultation process have contended that a
disadvantage of cost recovery is that it would
result in employer and labour groups relying on
different sources of data, thereby prolonging the
collective bargaining process.

The study team recommends to the Task Force
that the government consider recovering a portion

of the costs of the Pay Research Bureau directly from users, on the grounds of fairness and to provide a market test for the value of the services that the bureau provides.

Canadian Human Rights Commission (CHRC)

The CHRC administers the Canadian Human Rights Act which prohibits acts of discrimination on 10 grounds and applies to federal departments and agencies, and private companies under federal jurisdiction. The CHRC performs a unique variety of functions. It issues guidelines for compliance with the Act, investigates complaints, appoints conciliators, approves or rejects settlements, and in certain cases seeks the establishment of an independent tribunal which adjudicates on a case. As well, the Commission provides information to the public with the aim of reducing discrimination. It also lends its counsel to a complainant appearing before a tribunal and appears before a tribunal itself to argue in the "public interest".

In its report, the Study Team on Regulatory Programs observed that because of the scope of the CHRC's roles (as advocate, referee, and enforcer), "its activities are viewed with apprehension by the regulated who contend that there is insufficient regard for the costs or difficulties involved in compliance". The report further indicated employer concerns that their rights over the management of human resources are too severely restricted, that CHRC seems to be biased in favour of complainants, and stated that delay and uncertainty are substantive issues.

Our private sector consultation process confirms that a large number of employers -- both large and small -- question the basic fairness of the CHRC's process and believe that it is unduly biased in favour of the complainant. A few of those consulted suggested that the CHRC should be abolished, and that henceforth discrimination complaints should be dealt with by the courts. However, the majority of employers consulted were of the view that the Commission be maintained but that steps be taken to ensure that complainants and defendants are treated equally.

Our observations with respect to the CHRC are as follows:

a. Some of the concerns regarding the CHRC process have been addressed in the recent amendments to the Human Rights Act (Bill C-27, enacted in June 1985). In particular, when the Commission determines that a complaint is substantial, it no longer is responsible for appointing the members of the tribunal which adjudicates on the case. The process followed by the investigators, who are frequently perceived by employers as favouring the complainant, is now included in the regulations and made subject to approval by Cabinet.

b. Much concern has been expressed that complainants do not bear any portion of the costs associated with processing complaints.

c. In the consultations, many complaints have been raised regarding substantial delays in processing complaint applications before the CHRC.

d. The study team agrees with those in the consultation process who expressed the view that it is unfair to a defendant for the CHRC to publicly disclose a complaint prior to any formal consideration of the complaint by the Commission. Publication of what may be a frivolous or vexatious complaint could cause serious and unjustified damage to the reputation of an individual or goodwill of an employer.

The study team recommends to the Task Force that the government consider implementing on a priority basis the previous proposals relating to cost awards and maximum time limits for disposing of complaint applications.

Integration of the Tariff Board, Canadian Import Tribunal and Textile and Clothing Board

The government announced a decision-in-principle to integrate the Tariff Board, Canadian Import Tribunal and the Textile and Clothing Board, in May, 1985. The statement read as follows:

"There are similarities in the mandates of several import review bodies and much of the expertise needed to carry out their functions can be shared. The government is therefore proposing to integrate the Canadian Import Tribunal, the Tariff Board and the Textile and Clothing Board. The 'court of easy access' facility of the present Tariff Board will be preserved. Ministers will be developing a detailed proposal to implement this decision-in-principle."

Key implementation issues with respect to the proposed integration of the three import bodies relate to the functions that should be included, and how they should be organized. An

interdepartmental committee of officials is
currently addressing these issues in the context
of developing a detailed implementation plan.
Based on our consultations, the study team has
made the following observations which it hopes
will be helpful in the development of this plan:

a.   All of the inquiry functions currently
      performed by the three import bodies
      should be included in the new body. In
      this regard, we note that all three
      bodies presently have two types of
      inquiry functions, relating to general
      economic inquiries and specific material
      injury inquiries.

b.   A case can be made, within the context
      of designing the proposed new tribunal,
      for establishing a separate panel to
      deal with questions of material injury
      in relation to dumped or subsidized
      goods and services, particularly if such
      questions (which are presently dealt
      with by the Canadian Import Tribunal)
      are expected to become increasingly
      important in the context of the
      forthcoming round of GATT negotiations
      during which the reduction of barriers
      to trade in services will be expressly
      addressed. It may also be desirable to
      consider establishing separate panels to
      deal with matters relating to the
      current activities of the Textile and
      Clothing Board and the Tariff Board.

c.   An important issue relates to whether
      the appellate function currently
      performed by the Tariff Board should be
      included in the proposed new import
      body. The appellate function is
      judicial in nature, involving the
      interpretation of customs laws on

appeals from Revenue Canada rulings
regarding the classification and value
for duty of imported goods. This
function bears little resemblance to the
conduct of injury inquiry investigations
or general inquiries. The proposals
presently being developed to restructure
the Tax Court of Canada with a two-tier
system could afford an opportunity to
transfer the appellate function to the
lower and less formal tier of that
proposed system. The study team
believes that a strong case can be made
for retaining the appellate function in
the proposed new import body. In this
regard, industry appears to be generally
satisfied with the manner in which this
function has been carried out, that
companies particularly like the 'court
of easy access' approach by the Tariff
Board, and that the government has made
a commitment to maintain this approach.

The study team recommends to the Task Force
that the government consider maintaining the
appellate function currently performed by the
Tariff Board in the proposed new import body,
unless it can be clearly demonstrated that
transferring this function to the proposed
two-tier Tax Court will preserve the 'court of
easy access' approach followed by the Tariff
Board.

REGULATORY AGENCIES AND REGULATORY REFORM

CONCLUDING OBSERVATIONS

As noted previously, this report does not address the total package of regulatory reform issues. The study team has focussed on regulatory agencies in the context of their relationship with government. As directed in the terms of reference, the study team has dealt with issues of process, rather than content. The study team has noted that other significant regulatory reform issues -- relating to the content of regulation and to the delivery of regulatory programs by departments -- have been addressed by the Study Team on Regulatory Programs.

In concluding this report, the study team makes two observations with respect to the role of regulatory agencies within the wider context of regulatory reform generally.

The study team is of the opinion that the adoption by the government of a general policy on regulatory intervention announced in the form of a statement of regulatory principles, as proposed by the Study Team on Regulatory Programs, could provide an over-all context within which to implement many of the proposals in this report. In this regard, we recognize that our suggestions designed to limit the role of agencies in policy making -- through periodic mandatory reviews of agency mandates, policy directives, and a stronger role for the government in approving agency regulations -- will be effective as the government and Parliament takes a more active role in regulatory policy development.

If the government wishes to adopt a general policy on regulatory intervention, in the study team's view it would be important to consider carefully the differences, as well as the similarities, between departments and agencies as instruments for performing regulatory functions. Based on the suggested general framework for defining the role of regulatory agencies, the study team has proposed that they should be limited as much as possible to adjudicative decision-making functions on specific matters, and they should retain a considerable degree of independence from the government with respect to the performance of such decision-making functions. If this approach is accepted, it follows that the principles governing the accountability of regulatory agencies must differ from those of government departments, particularly for decision-making. In the view of the study team, this should be explicitly recognized in defining the role of regulatory agencies within the broader context of Canadian regulatory policy.

RECORD OF CONSULTATION

Phillip Lynd   Rogers Telecommunications
                            Toronto

Beverly Briggs   Consultant
                            Pickering

Prof. Hudson Janisch   Lawyer
                            Toronto

Keith Dixon   Canadian Importers
                                Association
                            Toronto

Meline Batten   Canadian Radio Common
                                Carriers Association
                            Toronto & St. John's

Jacques Proulx   MS Mirable Services
                            Montreal

Nicole Lemieux   Hydro Québec
                            Montreal

Michèle Gouin   Hemens Harris
                            Montreal

Bernard Cloutier   Regie de l'électricité
                                et du gaz
                            Montreal

John Carty &   CP Air
    W.G. Endicott &   Vancouver
    G. Manning

Jack McMahon   Transwest Helicopters
                                Port Coquitlam

John Lutes   Lawyer
                                Vancouver

Peter Butler   Lawyer
                                Vancouver

Justice Gibbs   Vancouver

J.G. Stabback   Royal Bank of Canada
                                Calgary

Don McDougall   Custom Helicopter
                                Calgary

Darshan S. Kailly   Canadian Freightways
                                Calgary

Art Price   Independent Petroleum
                                Association
                                Calgary

John Rooke   Lawyer
                                Calgary

John Major   Lawyer
                                Calgary

Dennis Hart   Lawyer
                                Calgary

Robert P. Engle   Northwest Territorial
                           Airways
                       Yellowknife

Jack Heath   NWT Public Utilities Board
                       Yellowknife

Dennis Prince   Yukon Chamber of Mines
                       Whitehorse

Bill Dunbar   NorthwestTel
                       Whitehorse

Marvin Taylor   White Pass and Yukon
                           Corporation
                       Whitehorse

Ken MacKinnon   Northern Television Systems
                       Whitehorse

Joe Sparling   Air North Charter and
                           Training
                       Whitehorse

Diane Granger   Yukon Water and Utilities
                           Board
                       Whitehorse

Ross Priest   Carpenters Union Local 2499
                       Whitehorse

Joe Muff   Alkan Air
                       Whitehorse

Prof. John Meisel   Queen's University
                       Kingston

Jim Bennett	Canadian Federation of Independent Business Willowdale
Lynne Hall	Consultant Toronto
Ken Culver	Rio Algom Limited Toronto
Dr. Norman Aspin & J.E. Wilson	Canadian Nuclear Association Toronto
Brian Armstrong	Lawyer Toronto
John K. Archambault	TransCanada Pipeline Ltd. Toronto
Eleanore Smith	Lawyer Toronto
Prof. Reine Peterson	York University Toronto
Jim Conrad	Consultant Toronto
Peter S. Grant	Lawyer Toronto
David Bond & Pierre Nadeau & Wayne Stacey	Canadian Association of Broadcasters Ottawa

Al Kapty   Trans North Air
                            Whitehorse

Burrell W. Flower   Canadian UK Freight
                                Conference
                            Montreal

          Colombo   Federal Employers in
                                Transportation and
                                Communication Organizations
                            Montreal

onald G. Schmidt &   Corporation Provost Ltée.
   R.A. LeBlanc   Montreal

ernie Saunders &   Bell Canada
   R. Fenton   Montreal

Rick Richard &   Acadia Air
   Jim O'Shanahan   Halifax

Ian Kilpatrick   Newfoundland Capital
                                Corporation
                            Dartmouth

Ellwood Dillman   Scotia Investments
                            Halifax

Prof. Richard Schultz McGill University
                            Montreal

Ken Maclaren   Canadian Trucking
                                Association
                            Ottawa

Ken McDonald &   Canadian Consumers
    David McKendrick   Association
                        Ottawa

Michael Hind-Smith &   Canadian Cable Television
    Suzanne Cornell   Association
                        Ottawa

M. Kynes   Pollution Probe
                        Ottawa

Rodney Bell   Monserco
                        Mississauga

Laurent Thibault &   Canadian Manufacturers
    Graham Hughes   Association
                        Toronto

Mr. Pappalardo &   City Express
    R. Wedge &   Toronto
    J.T. Bulger

J. McCracken   Board of Trade of Metro
                            Toronto
                        Toronto

Colin Campbell   Lawyer
                        Toronto

Doug Gray   Lawyer
                        Toronto

C.R.O. Munro   C.P. Limited
                        Montreal

Charles Sirois	Télésystème National Québec
Melville Baillet	Loomis Courier Vancouver
John Trickett	Consoltex Montreal
Tass Grivakes	Lawyer Montreal
Dick Martin	Canada Labour Congress Ottawa
Ian Smythe	Canadian Petroleum Association Ottawa
Geoffrey Hale	Canadian Organization of Small Business Toronto
Dale Botting	CFIB Regina
Sam Horton	Ontario Hydro Toronto
J. Donnelly & Terence Wardrop	Atomic Energy Ottawa
Ian McNabb & Glen Hills	Canada Gas Association Ottawa

Andrew Roman   Canadian Public Advocacy
                                   Institute Energy Probe
                                Toronto

Eric Barry &   Canadian Textile Institute
   Tim Page &   Ottawa
   Elizabeth Siwicki

G.P. MacPherson   Corporation House Ltd.
                                Ottawa